My Holiday in

Australia

Jane Bingham

Published in paperback in 2014 by Wayland
Copyright © Wayland 2014

Wayland
338 Euston Road
London NW1 3BH

Wayland Australia
Level 17/207 Kent Street
Sydney NSW 2000

Produced for Wayland by

White Thomson Publishing Ltd
www.wtpub.co.uk
+44 (0)843 2087 460

Senior Editor: Victoria Brooker
Editors: Jane Bingham/Steve White-Thomson
Designer: Ian Winton
Map artwork: Stefan Chabluk
Proofreader: Alice Harman

British Library Cataloguing in Publication Data
Bingham, Jane
   My holiday in Australia
   1. Vacations – Australia – Juvenile literature
   2. Australia – Juvenile literature.
   I. Title II. Australia
   919.4'0472

   ISBN 978 07502 8312 0

Wayland is a division of Hachette Children's Books,
an Hachette UK company.

Printed in China

10 9 8 7 6 5 4 3 2 1

Cover: Sydney harbour: Shutterstock/Taras Vyshna;
Koala: Shutterstock/Cloudia Newland.

p.1: Shutterstock/melissaf84; p.5: Shutterstock/
Xavier MARCHANT; p.6: Shutterstock/MaszaS; p.7:
Shutterstock/CSLD; p.8: Shutterstock/Steven Bostock;
p.9: Dreamstime/Christopher Meder; p.10: Dreamstime/
Dennis Dolkens; p.11: Dreamstime/Robyn Mackenzie;
p.12: Shutterstock/Taras Vyshna; p.13: Shutterstock/
Christopher Meder; p.14: Dreamstime/Robyn Mackenzie;
p.15: Shutterstock/Debra James; p.16: Shutterstock/Yuri
Acurs; p.17: Dreamstime/Pi3rrhuang; p.18: Shutterstock/
Melissaf84; p.19 (top): Shutterstock/Markus Gebauer;
p.19 (bottom): Shutterstock/Allsop; p.20: Shutterstock/
Guido Amrein, Switzerland; p.21: Dreamstime/
Pi3rrhuang;p.22: Dreamstime/Hotshotsworldwide; p.23
(top): Shutterstock/Cloudia Newland; p.23 (middle):
Shutterstock/Four Oaks; p.23 (bottom): Dreamstime/
Gazah; p.24: Dreamstime/Chee-onn Leong; p.25:
Shutterstock/oliveromg; p.26: Shutterstock/Tan, Kim
Pin; p.27 (top): Shutterstock/GTS Production; p.27
(bottom): Dreamstime/Liumantiger; p.28:Shutterstock/
MaszaS; p.29: Shutterstock/Neale Cousland; p.30 (top):
Dreamstime/Deboracilli; p.30 (bottom):Dreamstime/
Jkerrigan.

Contents

This is Australia!

Australia is a very large country surrounded by sea. It is hundreds of miles away from any other country, so most visitors arrive by aeroplane.

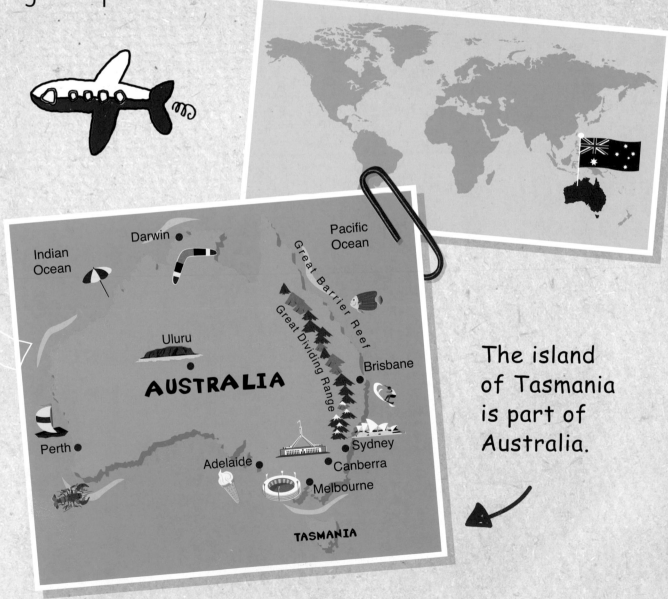

The island of Tasmania is part of Australia.

This is how Sydney looks from the air. The city was built around an enormous bay.

Many people fly to Sydney. It is a great place to start your Australian holiday.

It was a long flight to Australia, but I felt really happy when I saw Sydney!

Australian words: when you arrive

hello/hi
g'day (gud-ay)

Australian person
Aussie (oz-ee)

British person
Pom

5

A sunny country

The sun often shines in Australia. From December to February it is summertime and the weather is extremely hot. From June to August it is wintertime. It gets quite cold in the south, but most parts of Australia stay warm and sunny.

In northern Australia, you can swim in the sea all year round.

Things to take
- sun cream
- sun hat
- swimming costume

In the centre of Australia there are deserts that stretch for hundreds of miles. During the day, it is scorching hot in the desert. At night, the temperature drops very sharply.

Some Australian deserts have amazing red sand.

We took a trip to see the desert. It was baking hot and we had to drink lots of water.

A place to stay

There are lots of hotels along the coast near Brisbane.

Many visitors to Australia stay in a seaside hotel or rent an **apartment** close to the sea.

It only took three minutes to get from our hotel to the sea!

The land away from the coast is called the **outback**. Some families go camping in the outback.

These people have found a good place to camp underneath some **eucalyptus trees**.

Camping kit

- sleeping bag
- warm top
- torch

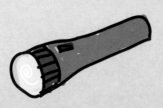

On the move

If you want to explore Australia, you will have to travel thousands of miles. You can take a coach or a train, but the quickest way to travel is by aeroplane.

Small passenger planes fly to some of the islands off the coast.

Australian cities have some interesting forms of transport. In Sydney, people catch a ferry across the harbour. In Brisbane, a fast motor boat takes you on the river to the city centre.

In Melbourne, you can catch a tram. Trams get their power from overhead electric cables.

Stunning cities

Australia has five large cities — Sydney, Melbourne, Brisbane, Perth and Adelaide. They are all busy places with a mixture of old and new buildings.

You will never be bored in Sydney! You can visit a museum, a park or a market, take a tour of the famous Opera House, or just relax on a beautiful beach.

We saw bats hanging from the trees in the Sydney **Botanical Gardens**. They looked scary!

Canberra is the capital city of Australia. It was built 90 years ago to be the home of the Australian government.

At night, the **parliament** building in Canberra is lit up.

City treats

Test your sporting skills – at Melbourne's National Museum of Sport

Meet sharks face to face – at the Sea Life Sydney Aquarium

Learn about Australian history – at the Museum of Australia in Canberra

Amazing sights

Australia has some amazing natural wonders. One of the most astonishing sights is Uluru, an enormous rocky mound in the Central Desert. At sunrise and sunset, it looks bright red!

Uluru is a **sacred** place for the **Aboriginal people**.

First people

The Aboriginals were the first people to live in Australia. Their history dates back over 50,000 years.

The Great Barrier Reef lies beneath the Pacific Ocean, off the northeast coast of Australia. It is made of coral – a hard, rocky substance formed from the skeletons of sea creatures.

The Great Barrier Reef is home to thousands of different types of fish.

We went in a glass-bottomed boat to look at the reef. I saw a turtle and some beautiful fish!

15

In the country

Away from the cities, there are farmlands, mountains, lakes and deserts. There is also a lot of unfarmed land covered by tough grass, bushes and trees. This wild countryside is known as 'the bush'.

There are some great walks through the bush, but watch out for snakes!

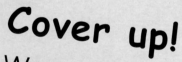

Cover up!

Wear long trousers and socks and shoes on a bush walk. They will help protect you from snakes!

Over half of Australia's land is used for farming. As you travel around the countryside, you will see some enormous sheep farms.

Some Australian farmers welcome visitors. You can stay on their farm and learn about their way of life.

This farm is on the island of Tasmania.

At the beach

This is Bondi Beach in Sydney. It is a great place to relax after seeing the sights.

Australia is famous for its beautiful sandy beaches and its sparkling blue sea.

Australian words: at the beach

swimming costume
cossie (**coz**-ee)

flip-flops
thongs

sunglasses
sunnies

Some of the world's best surfing beaches are in Australia.

These surfers are taking part in a contest on the east coast.

You don't need to be an expert to enjoy the waves. You can have lots of fun on a **boogie board**.

19

Original Australians

In the past, the Aboriginal people survived by hunting animals and gathering food. Today, some Aboriginals still keep up their ancient **traditions** and explain them to visitors.

This Aboriginal woman is preparing fruit to eat.

Aboriginal artists create striking paintings. Many of their paintings show the **Ancestor Spirits**. The Aboriginal people believe that these spirits created everything in the natural world.

This painting shows the Turtle Ancestor Spirit.

Aboriginal words

boomerang
curved hunting stick thrown at animals

didgeridoo
musical instrument made from a hollowed-out tree trunk or branch

billabong
small pond

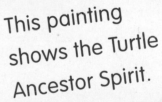

21

Watching wildlife

You will see some very unusual creatures on your holiday. Some Australian animals, such as kangaroos and koalas, are not found in the wild in any other country.

Kangaroos carry their babies in a pouch. The babies are often known as joeys.

I saw a kangaroo and her joey when we were in the outback. The joey looked so sweet!

These are just some of the creatures you can spot in Australia:

Koalas live in eucalyptus trees.

The laughing kookaburra sounds like someone laughing at a joke.

Rainbow lorikeets are incredibly colourful.

Feeling hungry

There is such good food to choose from in Australia! You can enjoy lots of fresh fruit and vegetables, and delicious meat and fish.

Australians eat a lot of seafood. Prawns and lobster taste really good with salad and mayonnaise.

Australian families love to cook outside on a barbecue. You might be invited to join in too!

On the menu

lamington
a sponge cake coated in chocolate icing and coconut flakes

pavlova
a meringue base filled with cream and fresh fruit

kangaroo meat
kangaroo tastes rather like chicken!

Shopping time

Australia has all kinds of shops, but if you want to buy something unusual, try a visit to a craft market.

This craft market is just beside the Sydney Harbour Bridge.

Aboriginal artists create paintings and hand-made objects that visitors can buy.

Boomerangs are popular **souvenirs**. They are decorated with traditional Aboriginal patterns.

You will need to pay with Australian dollars.

Be a sport!

Australia is a great place for outdoor activities. At the seaside, you can try out surfing, snorkelling or sailing. In the countryside, you can go cycling, canoeing or horse riding.

The warm waters of northern Australia are the perfect place for snorkelling.

Australians play a kind of soccer called Australian Rules Football. Try to see a game while you are on holiday – there is lots of action and the crowd gets very noisy!

I couldn't understand all the rules at the football match, but it was very exciting!

Make it yourself

Some Aboriginal paintings are made by painting lots of dots very close together. Why not try making your own dot painting?

These animal pictures were created in an Aboriginal style, using painted dots.

Step 1.
Draw the outline of an animal, such as a turtle, a lizard or a fish. Keep its shape very simple.

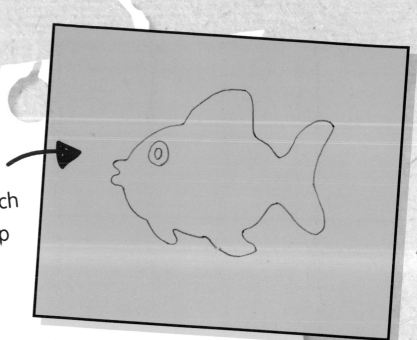

Step 2.
Draw faint lines round your animal shape. Then draw shapes to fill up the corners of the page. Paint coloured dots along your lines.

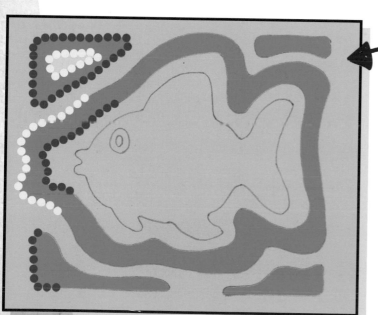

Step 3.
Fill in your animal's body with more lines and dots.

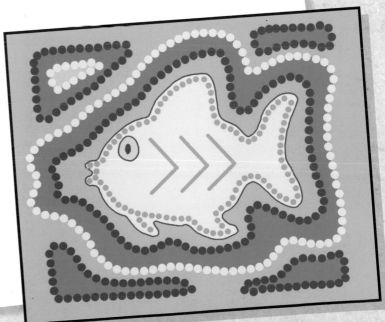

Useful words

Aboriginal people
The native people of Australia. The Aboriginal people have lived in Australia for over 50,000 years.

Ancestor Spirits
The spirits of the ancient ancestors of the Aboriginal people. Aboriginal people believe that the Ancestor Spirits created their land and all the people and animals in it.

apartment
A place where families can stay, with bedrooms, a bathroom, a kitchen and a living room.

boogie board
A small surfboard that you lie on to ride waves.

botanical gardens
Gardens where rare plants and trees grow.

eucalyptus trees
Trees with white bark and pale green leaves that grow in many parts of Australia. Eucalyptus trees are also called gum trees.

outback
The wild countryside away from the coast in Australia.

parliament
A group of people who are chosen to run a country.

sacred
Holy, or belonging to spirits and gods.

souvenir
Something that you buy to remind you of a holiday.

traditions
Actions that have been done in the same way for many years.